D0513876

The Hunter Story

The Hunter Story

Martin W. Bowman

The
History
Press

Published in the United Kingdom in 2009 by
The History Press
The Mill · Brimscombe Port · Stroud · Gloucestershire · GL5 2QG

Copyright © Martin W. Bowman, 2009

All rights reserved. No part of this publication may be
reproduced, stored in a retrieval system, or transmitted, in any
form, or by any means, electronic, mechanical, photocopying,
recording or otherwise, without the prior permission of the
publisher and copyright holder.

Martin W. Bowman has asserted the moral right to be identified
as the author of this work.

British Library Cataloguing in Publication Data
A catalogue record for this book is available from the British
Library.

Hardback ISBN 978-0-7524-5082-7

Typesetting and origination by The History Press
Printed in Italy

Half title page: *Formation of FGA.9 and Harrier
GR1 aircraft from RAF Wittering in 1973. (Richard
Wilson)*

Title page: *From a humble beginning as an F.4 in
1955, WV386 went on to serve with UK-based
units and, following a long period in storage, was
converted to T.75A standard for the RSAF and flown
out to Singapore in 1972. Retired in 1994, it was
purchased by Steve Appleton in the USA where it
underwent a complete rebuild which included the
fitting of a glass cockpit and an 11,250lb thrust
Avon-208 engine from a Sea Vixen. Repainted in
Black Arrows livery, it is currently based at Boise
with the serial number N81827. (Steve Appleton)*

CONTENTS

*F.6 XG253/A of 66
Squadron en route to
Iraq on 7 May 1957.
(Alastair Aked)*

INTRODUCTION

➤

Hunters of 237 OCU at RAF Lyneham on 2 August 1991, the last Hunters in RAF service. No.237 OCU had been established in 1971 for RAF pilots who were to convert to the Blackburn Buccaneer S.2, the two-seat Hunters providing an Integrated Flight Instrumentation System (IFIS) as a link between the Hawk advanced trainer and the operational Buccaneers at RAF Honington. (Adrian Balch)

If ever there was a real pilot's aeroplane it was the Hunter, an outstanding multi-purpose aircraft which excelled in the roles of interceptor fighter, ground attack, reconnaissance, research vehicle and two-seater trainer, and not forgetting the dramatic formation aerobatic performances.

British fighters had been among the world's finest during the Second World War. Many of them, such as the Hawker Hurricane and the Typhoon rocket-firing fighter, were the result of the design teams headed by Sydney Camm, a man who had been Hawker's Chief Designer since 1925. His greatest post-war creation, the Hunter, beckoned, but bringing this project (and others) to fruition would prove difficult. Work on the Hunter commenced late in 1948, but because of the depressed post-war economic situation in Britain, it was not until early 1950 that Hunter prototypes were constructed. Neville Duke made the first flight on 20 July 1951, and on 19 September 1953 he piloted a Hunter to shatter the world air speed record.

The Hunter is one of the world's greatest aircraft which for three decades pilots enthused about, extolling the smooth, aerodynamic lines, 4 x 30mm cannon, the Rolls-Royce Avon engine, and its outstandingly honest handling characteristics combined with a lively performance. Who can ever forget the glory days of the unforgettable aerobatic displays with the Black Knights, Black Arrows and Blue Diamonds? It vividly recalls operations in Europe with Fighter Command and 2nd TAF, in Cyprus, the Middle East and the Far East, where Hunters in the ground-attack

role operated against rebels in Aden and Malaysia respectively.

The Hunter was undoubtedly a classic thoroughbred of its time from the stables of one of the finest fighter manufacturers in the world. The Hunter's success assured, for fifty years its longevity and adaptability was rarely challenged, the last example being retired in July 2001. The Hunter legend lives on, however, with some 114 potentially airworthy airframes located in fourteen countries around the world.

Did you know?

In June 1962 when the RAF won the NATO AIRCENT gun-firing competition for the first time, Shiny Blue used Hunter F.6s and their 30mm cannon to eclipse RCAF Sabres, which traditionally used .5in machine-guns to win this competition in the past. The .5in machine-gun was much easier to harmonize and the Sabre was a very stable gun platform. The Hunter was a 'livelier' aircraft and the 30mm cannon was 'quite a handful'.

In Britain in November 1946, the specification for the first swept-wing jet, powered by the 5,000lb-thrust Nene 2, was issued. Eight months earlier, three prototypes of Hawker Aircraft's first jet fighter, the P.1040, which was adapted for carrier-based interception, had been ordered. The first P.1040 prototype flew on 2 September 1947, powered by a 4,500lb-thrust Rolls-Royce Nene I, which produced a maximum speed of about Mach 0.77 (510mph). An increase in speed and performance only resulted when Camm forged ahead with plans for a swept-wing design, designated the P.1047, powered by a more powerful Nene engine. The new wings had a sweepback of 35°on the quarter chord and a thickness ratio of 0.10. By the end of 1947, Sydney Camm and his design team at Richmond Road, Kingston-upon-Thames knew they would have to design an aircraft that could accommodate the new 6,500lb Rolls-Royce A.J.65 axial-flow turbojet. This engine would soon become world famous as the Avon. Specification F.3/48 was issued to Hawkers early in 1948 for a single-seat, cannon-armed, day interceptor fighter capable of Mach 0.94 (620mph at 36,000ft, 724mph at sea level) and have an endurance of sixty minutes. An ejection seat would be mandatory and provision had to be made for a future radar-ranging gunsight. The main characteristics of Camm's original P.1067 design included an Avon engine mounted in the fuselage amidships with annular nose air intake and exhausting through a long jet pipe in the extreme tail. The wing was swept back 42½° on the quarter-chord and a straight-tapered tailplane was mounted

Did you know?
In the early 1950s air-firing trials identified a need to fit a housing to collect spent cartridge cases and links that might otherwise damage the airframe. Two blister fairings, which the RAF knew as 'Sabrinas' after an unusually well-endowed young starlet, cured the problem. Swiss Hunters were said to have enlarged 'Sabrinas' for weapons training, collecting both links and cases.

on top of the fin, though this was later deleted.

The P.1067 was the only single-seat, single-engined fighter in the world designed to carry four cannon. But indecision surrounded both the choice of gun and the engine to power the P.1067. Finally in 1949, four 30mm Aden cannon armament fit was adopted, cleverly mounted with their magazines in a removable gun-pack located behind the cockpit. WB188, the first of the three prototypes and WB195 were powered by the Avon, while the Armstrong-Siddeley Sapphire powered WB202. This aircraft went on to become the prototype Hunter F.2.

Hawkers would build 139 Avon-powered F.1s and Armstrong-Whitworth forty-five Sapphire-engined Mk 2s before production switched to the F.4.

◄◄
Hawker Hunters in production in the mid-1950s. In the background are the front and centre sections of the P.1121 supersonic strike fighter prototype. (BAe)

◄
Work in progress on the first prototype P.1067 WB188 approaching completion in experimental works at Richmond Road. (BAe)

Work on the three prototypes continued throughout 1950–51. WB188 was painted a glossy, pale duck-egg green finish and on 1 July 1951, Chief Test Pilot Sqn Ldr Neville Duke carried out WB188's first engine run. On 20 July he flew the prototype on a forty-seven-minute flight and two months later, Duke was making high-speed passes in excess of 700mph at the Farnborough Air Show.

On 5 May 1952 Duke flew WB195, the second P.1067, now officially called 'Hunter', from the new Hawker test field at Dunsfold, Surrey. WB195 differed

from WB188 in having a production R.A. (Reheated Avon) 7 and full military equipment, including four Aden cannon and radar ranging gunsight. On 4 June, Neville Duke put WB195 through its paces at West Raynham in front of the RAF's Central Fighter Establishment, which would be the first to receive production Hunters prior to their entry into squadron service. On 10 July 1952 Duke flew WB188 at the Brussels Air Show in front of a large and very appreciative crowd. The Hunter's triumphant public debut was at that year's September SBAC show at Farnborough, where WB195 was flown each day with WB188 held in reserve. The occasion was overshadowed by the loss on 6 September of the de Havilland DH.110 prototype, its pilot, John Derry, and his fellow crewmember Anthony Richards. Thirty

Sqn Ldr Neville Duke in the cockpit of P.1067 Hunter prototype WB188 in front of the flight sheds at Dunsfold in 1951. (BAe)

Did you know?

In 1956 120 Hunter F.50 single-seaters (J 34) were delivered to the Flygvapnet (Swedish Air Force) but no two-seat aircraft accompanied the large order.

P.1067 Hunter prototype WB188 in flight. (BAe)

Did you know?

1,972 Hunter aircraft flew in forty RAF and five Royal Navy squadrons and nineteen overseas air forces.

people on the ground were killed and sixty-three people were injured. In spite of the tragedy, Neville Duke followed with a truly brilliant flying display, which included a transonic dive. Duke flew WB202, the third P.1067 prototype, for the first time on 30 November 1952.

It was evident that having just the three prototypes was woefully inadequate, and the first twenty production Hunter F.1s came to be regarded as development machines, being used to test numerous trial installations including an area-ruled fuselage, blown flaps and alternative styles of air brake. Limited fuel capacity reduced the F.1 endurance substantially and there was the problem of rapid pitch up, which began to occur in some manoeuvres at the higher subsonic Mach numbers without adequate warning. There were

severe compressor surge problems with the Avon 104 and to a lesser extent, the Mk 113 engine. Engine surging noticeably increased when gun gases were ingested during high-altitude gun firing. Diving to increase airspeed and to reduce altitude usually affected recovery from the surge, but engine flame out often resulted. These problems were finally eliminated with the introduction of the surge-free R.A.21. The 8,000lb-thrust Sapphire 101-engined Hunter F.2 had no such engine surge problems, and gun firing was cleared up to 47,000ft. Also, the Sapphire, as fitted to the F.2, could develop slightly more thrust at a lower specific fuel consumption than the Avon, as fitted to the F.1. Even so, except for 105 Sapphire-powered F.5s, Avon engines powered all the Hunters in service. Frank Murphy flew WT555, the first production Hunter F.1, at Dunsfold on 16 May 1953, but the F.1 would not finally enter service until late in July 1954.

In 1953 WB188 was modified for an attempt to break the World Absolute Air Speed Record, which stood at 715.75mph set by an F-86D Sabre. In August WB188 was adapted to take an R.A.7R Avon, capable of 7,130lb thrust 'dry' and 9,600lb with reheat lit. The Hunter, which was painted bright red overall and designated the Mk 3, also received a sharply pointed nose-cone fairing and a windscreen fairing. Operating from Tangmere, Sussex on 7 September, Neville Duke made practice runs in WB188 along the 3km course off the coast of Rustington, achieving an average speed of 727.63mph (Mach 0.92 at sea level). On 19 September, Duke flew WB188 round a 100km closed circuit

to set a new world record for this course at 709.2mph. Shortly afterwards the Supermarine Swift broke Duke's record flying at 735.70mph in Libya, where higher ambient temperatures greatly assisted the record-breaking attempt.

The first of 365 F.4s flew on 20 October 1954. All were built with a 'full flying tail' and they were powered by the Avon R.A.7 rated 113 or 115, the latter modified to reduce engine surge. Fuel capacity was increased by the installation of bigger internal fuel cells and two 100-gallon drop tanks on inboard wing pylons. Provision was made for under-wing stores. The first of 105 Sapphire-powered Armstrong-Whitworth-built F.5s flew on 19 October 1954. After the scrapping of numerous F.4 and F.5 airframes during 1960–63, it became cost-effective to re-build F.4s to take the bigger, more powerful Avon 200-series engine. The P.1101 trainer prototype (XJ615) flew for the first time on 8 July 1955. The two-seater was powered by the same Avon 113 as fitted to the Hunter F.4, but the second prototype (XJ627), which was based on the F.6, and which flew on 17 November 1956, was powered by the more powerful Avon 203. This engine was not adopted on production aircraft however. The first T.7 production model (XL563) flew on 11 October 1957. The forty-five T.7s built differed from the fighter versions in having a nose lengthened by 3ft. At first the T.7 was armed with two cannon in the nose, but this was later reduced to just one gun with the deletion of the port Aden. During 1957–58, six more Hunter T.7s were converted from F.4 airframes and these were delivered between February and May 1959.

The Hunter F.6 was really a new aircraft designed as an interceptor, but developed with the ground-attack role in mind. It evolved from the P.1099, which was created by marrying updated production wings to the redundant P.1083 fuselage and installing the Rolls-Royce Avon R.A.14 engine, which by April 1952 was producing 10,500lb static thrust. Experienced Hunter pilots noticed the difference immediately. In addition to inboard 1,000lb bombs or 100-gallon drop tanks, four rocket tiers were

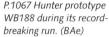

P.1067 Hunter prototype WB188 during its record-breaking run. (BAe)

Did you know?

Plans to produce a supersonic Hunter (P.1083), using an afterburning R.A.14 Avon engine and 50° swept-wing, ended on 13 July 1953 with the cancellation of the prototype. If the change in wing sweep had gone ahead, the P.1083 might well have achieved supersonic performance in level flight.

mounted under each outer wing so that up to twenty-four 3in rocket projectiles could be carried. Neville Duke flew the P.1099 prototype (XF833) on 23 January 1954. The new engine was then derated to 10,000lb static thrust and became the Avon 203. On 20 July 1954 P.1099 flight trials were resumed and were successful. Seven F.1 airframes were quickly converted to 'interim Mk 6' standard to serve as pre-production aircraft. Bill Bedford flew WW592, the first, on 25 March 1955. By mid-1956 just over 100 F.6s had been built. Early production models were fitted with a variable-incidence tailplane, just as on previous marks, but all subsequent F.6 models had a 'flying tail' and extended-chord dog-tooth wings.

A conversion contract to modify thirty-three Hunter F.6 aircraft to FR.10 standard for the reconnaissance role was received in 1958 to meet a need to replace the Supermarine Swift FR.5 in 2nd Tactical Air Force (2nd TAF) in Germany and the Meteor FR.9 in the Far East. The FR.10 differed principally from the F.6 in having three forward-looking reconnaissance cameras in the nose, where they replaced the radar ranging scanner and camera gun. Armour plating had to be fitted under the cockpit floor as ballast. The four Aden cannon were retained for a secondary air defence role if required. With 230-gallon drop tanks, the FR.10 could fly from Germany to Malta non-stop if required. XF429, the first conversion, flew for the first time on 7 November 1958. The Hunter F.4 had only a short career with the majority of squadrons in Germany but in 1960 Nos 2 and 4 Squadron's in 2nd TAF received

Hunter FR.10s to form RAF Germany's Tactical Reconnaissance Wing, which operated until 1970–71.

In May 1958 the first of forty-one Hunter T.8, -B and -C dual-control trainers for the Royal Navy's swept-wing carrier aircraft programme were delivered to 764 Training Squadron at RNAS Lossiemouth. F.4 WW664, which was converted to two-seat configuration, effectively became the prototype T.8, and twenty-seven first-phase T.8s followed. During 1958–59 eighteen F.4s were brought up to T.8 standard. In 1963 a Navy requirement for operational training on the Tactical Air Navigation (TACAN) system led to the delivery of four T.8B aircraft with full TACAN equipment. An order for ten F.4s to be converted to T.8C with partial TACAN equipment followed.

Did you know?

On 8 February 1956 six of the eight pilots in the Day Fighter Leaders' School (DFLS) at RAF West Raynham, Norfolk who were briefed for a four versus four dogfight in their Hunter F.1s, crashed, out of fuel and in bad weather, while trying to land. The first pair managed to land, the No.2's engine flaming out on the runway. One pilot was killed. Another, too low to eject, force-landed straight ahead, finishing up in a hedge beside a road. Four others ejected safely.

▼

Hunter F.1 of the AFDS flying over RAF West Raynham, Norfolk by Flt Lt Duncan Simpson, who later became a Harrier test pilot with Hawkers. (CFE)

In July 1954 about twelve newly modified Hunter F.1s were issued to the CFE at West Raynham and 43 Squadron at RAF Leuchars. Scotland began receiving its first Hunter F.1s, becoming fully operational by October. Late in 1954 and early in 1955, four more first-line squadrons received Hunter F.1s and F.2s. The engine surge problems associated with the F.1 restricted all other deliveries to Operational Conversion Units (OCUs). The Empire Test Pilots School at RAE Farnborough and the Fighter Weapons School at Leconfield, Yorkshire also operated F.1s and F.2s.

In April 1955 Hunter F.4s began arriving at West Raynham for use with the Air Fighting Development Squadron (AFDS) and DFLS. During the year F.4s re-equipped three front-line squadrons and 229 OCU at Chivenor and the Flying College at Manby, Lincolnshire also took delivery of the F.4. In 2nd TAF the F.4 replaced all ten squadrons of Sabre F.1/F.4s in the Brüggen, Geilenkirchen, Jever, Oldenburg and Wildenrath wings, and the three DH Venom FB.1 Squadrons of the Fassberg Wing. The Jever Wing became the first in Germany to receive the Hunter F.4, eventually becoming a four-squadron Hunter wing operating in the dual role of air defence and ground attack.

Replacement of five squadrons of Sapphire-engined Hunter F.2s, Meteor F.8s and Swifts with Hunter F.5s occurred in 1955. By 1956 seven fighter squadrons were equipped with the Hunter F.4 in the UK and thirteen in 2nd Tactical Air Force. In October two squadrons of Hunter F.5s flew to Cyprus to be in position to provide top cover over Egypt for British and French aircraft involved in Operation *Musketeer*, the Anglo-French occupation of the Suez Canal zone. On 2 November the Hunters, carrying the yellow and black Suez identification stripes, began to cover sorties in support of naval fighter-bombers, but their limited endurance permitted only

Four Hunter F.1s of 54 Squadron's aerobatic team in 1955. (Via Bernard Noble)

◄◄
F.6 XG236/N of 66 Squadron en route to Baghdad in May 1957. Iraqi triangular wing and pre-Revolutionary fin flash markings replaced the RAF roundels and fin flashes, as it was to act as reserve aircraft for a fly-past in Baghdad. (Alastair Aked)

◄
F.6 XG253/A of 66 Squadron en route to Iraq on 7 May 1957. (Alastair Aked)

a short time over the patrol area. This and the Egyptian Air Force's almost total absence resulted in the Hunters being operated as base defence at Akrotiri and Nicosia, to deter possible incursions over Cyprus by Egyptian Il-28 bombers. No air-to-air encounters were reported and the Hunters returned to the UK.

In 1956 the first Hunter F.6s began re-equipping four squadrons in the UK, and seven more in 1957 when Duncan Sandys' infamous Defence White Paper predicted that the ICBM would shortly render manned interceptor aircraft obsolete. HM Government reduced the number of Hunter F.6s for the RAF by 100 aircraft and a 1955 order for fifty F.6s was cancelled. Nine of the thirteen Hunter F.4 squadrons in 2nd TAF were disbanded almost immediately. At Hawkers, the crisis of confidence caused by

In May 1957 eight 74 'Tiger' Squadron Hunters left RAF Horsham St Faith (now Norwich Airport) for Chièvres on an exchange with the Belgian Air Force, but before they left a photo opportunity was created by the presence in Norwich of Bertram Mills' Circus. (Ian Cadwallader)

Sandys' White Paper was largely overcome with the introduction of the ground-attack Hunter and F.4 production being further increased in the late 1950s and early 1960s to meet the needs of several overseas air forces. By the end of 1958 all Hunter squadrons in Fighter Command and the five F.4 Squadrons in Germany had completed re-equipment with Hunter F.6s. That same year, T.7s entered RAF service with 229

'Tiger' Squadron Hunters on the prowl. (Via Bob Cossey)

Did you know?

Apart from Britain, Hunters served overseas air forces including, India, Jordan, Iraq, Switzerland and Chile and no fewer than twenty-one countries purchased new and refurbished examples during 1954–75.

OCU at Chivenor. Later examples were issued to operational squadrons in Fighter Command and 2nd TAF in Germany. During 1958, heightened tension in Cyprus, Jordan and the Lebanon saw Hunters being based in Nicosia and these were often supported by detachments from the UK.

T.7 XL568 in the snow at Horsham St Faith in 1957. (Ian Cadwallader)

Flt Lt (later AVM) John Howe of 'C' Flight, 222 Squadron in front of F.4 WV327/U at Leuchars, Scotland in the summer of 1957. (Group Captain Ed Durham)

222 Squadron's F.4s lined up at RAF Leuchars in the summer of 1957. (Group Captain Ed Durham)

F.4 WV406/F of 222 Squadron at Leuchars, Scotland in the summer of 1957. (Group Captain Ed Durham)

F.6s of 26 Squadron, 124 Wing, 2nd TAF on the pan at RAF Gütersloh, West Germany in 1957. (Chris Cowper via Alan Pollock)

F.6s of 66 Squadron at RAF Acklington, Northumberland in late August 1958. (Alastair Aked)

FGA.9 at Dunsfold in 1958 showing the range of weapons available for the Hunter, although the Fireflash and Firestreak missiles to the rear at the wing tips did not enter operational service with the aircraft. (BAe)

A vast array of weapons available for the Hunter at Farnborough in 1959. (Ian Cadwallader)

The P.1101 trainer prototype (XJ615) at Farnborough on 11 September 1959. It flew for the first time on 8 July 1955. The two-seater was powered by the same Avon 113 as fitted to the Hunter F.4, but the second prototype (XJ627), which was based on the F.6, and which flew on 17 November 1956, was powered by the more powerful Avon 203. (Tom Trower)

➤ F.6 cockpit. (BAe)

➤➤ The distinctive tiger markings of F.6 XF511 of 74 Squadron at Horsham St Faith in 1960. 74 Squadron operated Hunters from 1957 to 1960. (Ray Deacon collection)

27

Did you know?

On 5 April 1968 Flt Lt Alan Pollock of No.1 Squadron crossed London and proceeded to put the power on as he passed the Houses of Parliament where a debate was in progress. Circling three times he levelled out over the Thames and dipped his wings in salute to the RAF Memorial and then approached Tower Bridge downstream at over 300mph in an adverse bomb run before flying through the 110ft deep x 200ft wide gap framed by its towers and bascules! Pollock subsequently received a medical discharge from the service.

'You're quite sure you're just going to BUZZ the Houses of Parliament?'

On 5 April 1968 Flt Lt Pollock of 1 Squadron flew F.6 XF442 'H-Hotel' across London and through Tower Bridge. The aircraft is pictured at the Lightning base at RAF Leconfield, Yorkshire in September 1965. (John Hale)

Two contemporary cartoons of the incident.

◄ *A Hunter of 2nd Tactical Air Force over Norway. (Dickie Dickinson)*

▲ *FGA.9s XJ683/F and XJ690/G of 20 Squadron from RAF Tengah, Singapore in 1965. (Richard Wilson)*

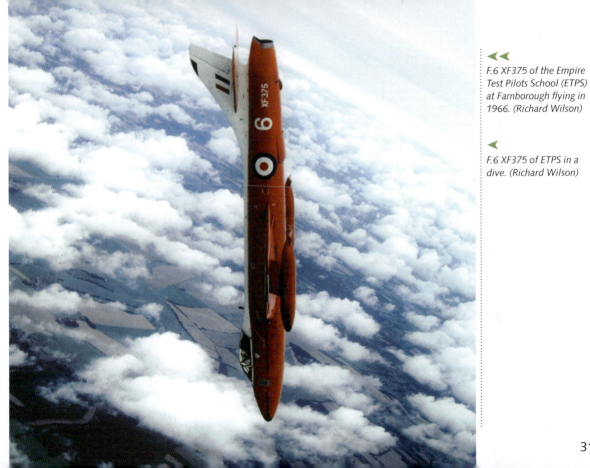

◄◄
F.6 XF375 of the Empire Test Pilots School (ETPS) at Farnborough flying in 1966. (Richard Wilson)

◄
F.6 XF375 of ETPS in a dive. (Richard Wilson)

<<

T.7 XL616 of the Empire Test Pilots School at Boscombe Down aloft in 1976. XL616 was flown for the first time on 3 January 1959. (Richard Wilson)

<

The Middle East Command's aerobatic team of four FGA.9s of 208 Squadron from RAF Eastleigh in 1960–61 with Mount Kilimanjaro in the background.

Did you know?

On 11 September 1973, during the military coup, Chilean Hunters maintained air cover over Concepción while other Hunters carried out rocket and cannon attacks on the President's house in Santiago and on his palace at La Moneda. Not one building outside the targets was hit.

33

An early morning sunrise at RAF Muharraq (Bahrain) in 1963 catches 8 Squadron FGA.9s being readied for an exercise. (Ray Deacon)

◄ *'Ginger' Rees marshalling a Hunter on the Khormaksar pan in Spring 1963. Terry McNally prepares to attach the access ladder and in the background Dave Waring is assisting an 8 Squadron pilot to strap-in. The Hunter pan at Khormaksar could hold twenty aircraft and was shared by three units at any one time. (Ray Deacon)*

◄ *Apart from the bowser driver, a buzz of activity is evident on the Khormaksar pan in early 1964, as 8 Squadron ground-crew set to work on turning round an FGA.9. The lack of squadron markings is due to the aircraft having recently returned from refurbishment in the UK. (Ray Deacon)*

35

Willie Marr and armourer colleague load an HE 60lb rocket to the outer rail of an 8/43 Squadron Hunter at Khormaksar in 1965, prior to a strike in the Adeni mountains. (Willie Marr, via Ray Deacon)

Between flights, the Hunters were turned-round, fully armed and fuelled-up in twenty minutes, so good teamwork was essential. Undoubtedly the hardest job on the line was changing the 30mm Aden gunpack, requiring three armourers and the assistance of a trusted Arab worker. In this view in the summer of 1963, 'Jock' Harmon (right) and Bob Cales lower a pack on an 8 Squadron FGA.9 at Khormaksar as the Arab collects the cannon links. (Ray Deacon)

Following the reformation of 1417 Flight in March 1963, a new unit pennant was produced and applied, initially, to the forward fuselage of the unit's four FR.10s. When centralised servicing was introduced in June 1964, it was also applied to the four T.7s. Number 1417 Flight operated Hunters from 1963 to 1967. (Ray Deacon)

The Hunter had a pressurised fuel system and, although fuel spillage was rare, it had to be tackled swiftly in the Aden heat to avoid a volatile incident. Here at Khormaksar early in 1964, airfield fire crews lay a blanket of foam as the Air/Sea Rescue Sycamore helicopter hovers nearby in case it is needed. (Ray Deacon)

Having been used on
tropical trials in Bahrain
in 1958, T.7, XL566
spent the next four years
with 43 Squadron at
Leuchars and Nicosia
before moving with the
unit to Aden. In this
1967 view the T.7 is
bearing the markings of
8 and 43 Squadron on
either side of the roundel
with the 1417 Flt flash
applied to the forward
fuselage. Following
the British withdrawal
from Aden in 1967
and the disbandment
of 1417 Flight and 43
Squadron, T.7, XL566
was reallocated to 208
Squadron at Muharraq.
(The Aviation Bookshop,
via Ray Deacon)

◄
T.7 XL572 of 229 OCU Chivenor on 22 August 1971. On 27 August 1959 XL572 took part in a spin demonstration and failed to recover. The CFS instructor ejected but was killed while the OCU instructor recovered from the spin and landed the aircraft safely. (Lawrie Reid)

◄◄
XF436-U, one of four FR.10s operated by 8 Squadron from April 1961 until March 1963, photographed outside the Hunter hangar in October 1962 following repair and repaint. (Ray Deacon)

▶

T.8M XL580 airborne in 1976. In June 1962 this Hunter became the 'Admiral's barge' when it was allocated to 764 Squadron FOFT (Flag Officer Flying Training) at RNAS Yeovilton. Note the admiral's pennant painted on the nose and the white surround applied to the national insignia. (HAL)

▶▶

T.8M XL602 climbing away from the camera ship. (BAe)

▲
T.8M XL719 wearing the famous 'Bunch with the Punch' markings of 899 Squadron, Royal Navy. Note the AIM-9L Sidewinder missile simulator on the outboard wing pylon. (Author)

➤
The Blue Herons aerobatic display team. In July 1975 four GA.11s flown by civilian pilots of Airwork Services and based at RNAS Yeovilton (otherwise known as HMS Heron) formed the Blue Herons aerobatic team, believed to be the first aerobatic team in the world in which civilian pilots flew military jet fighter aircraft. (Richard Wilson)

➤➤
Immaculate red Hunter T.7, part of the Fighter Jets Collection at Bournemouth in the 1990s. (Author)

G-BOOM, ex-Danish Air Force T.7 ET274 built by Fokker in Holland. (Author)

44

In the 1950s and early 1960s, the RAF team selected to give aerobatic displays did so whilst retaining a first-line operational capability. In 1956 'Treble One' Squadron, which were equipped with Hunter F.4s and commanded by Sqn Ldr Roger L. Topp AFC*, provided RAF Fighter Command's aerobatic reserve team. For the first time since the war, the RAF permitted an aerobatic team to paint its aircraft in a special display finish, and black was finally chosen. In 1956 a leading French newspaper had dubbed the team 'les Fleches Volantes', or 'Flying Arrows'. In June 1957 at the 22nd Paris Salon display, the team, which was the only one in Europe regularly flying five swept-wing aircraft, was described as 'les Fleches Noir', and the 'Black Arrows' were born. By the summer of 1958 jet-pipe smoke generators were fitted to the F.6s and thus the team was able to produce bold smoke trails to trace the pattern of its manoeuvres. That year the team flew most of their twenty-four major displays in seven countries with five Hunters, but there were rumours of a larger number of aircraft being flown by other air forces. The Black Arrows thought of a sixteen-plane formation, the squadron's full complement of aircraft. Then it was felt that they could make a really big impact at Farnborough in September with something even larger. Roger Topp considered many weird and wonderful shapes and eventually came up with twenty-one aircraft in seven echelons of three. But he felt that that there was something missing, so he added one more. They would go for a twenty-two Hunter loop!

Twenty-six serviceable Hunters were required, so extra pilots and Hunters had

Did you know?
As part of the development of the Tactical Strike Reconnaissance (TSR-2) nuclear bomber, a damaged Hunter F.6 fitted with a two-seat front section, modified to carry an advanced electronics and flight controls system, was to act as a training aircraft for the aircrews. Painted green and white, it was classified T.Mk 12. The TSR-2 was cancelled in 1964.

➤

Five Black Arrows in line abreast formation. (AM)

➤➤

Black Arrows in formation. (AM)

to be borrowed from other squadrons. Not every squadron wanted to give up their 'aces' or their best Hunters, but eventually the numbers were achieved. The twenty- two loop conceived by Topp was purely a build-up from doing something more than the sixteen and it more or less evolved as they tried to get something that made

sense to look at, had impact, and was feasible to fly. Twenty-two aircraft provided a spare aircraft within the formation. Once committed to the run in there was no way spares could be used, so if there was a failure everyone would move up their own line and the twenty-second aircraft could fill in the gap.

At Odiham on 1 September the team practiced in the morning and gave their first display that afternoon in front of 7,300 VIPs and guests in the trade stands at Farnborough. Roger Topp recalls 'going for the loop', which is published here for the first time:

A few minutes ago we took-off from Odiham in Hampshire, formed our glossy-black Hunter fighters into a tight arrowhead formation and headed for Farnborough.

◄◄
*The Black Arrows
practicing twenty-two
formation aerobatics. (Via
Tony Aldridge)*

◄
*Sixteen Black Arrows in
formation at Farnborough
in 1960. (Brian Allchin)*

49

Weeks of training in the relative obscurity of the Suffolk skies have prepared us for this occasion. Today is the start of the Farnborough Air Display, a world class air show, a big event. Our formation is big too, for we are about to demonstrate something audaciously new in the realm of fighter aerobatics; a loop by a formation of no less than twenty-two aircraft.

Rapidly we approach Farnborough, which lies dead ahead at four miles. Against the background of red-bricked houses forming the small township, the airfield stands out clearly and we can see the many brightly-polished parked aircraft, the blue and white striped awnings of the numerous marquees and the dark mass of the crowd.

Three miles to go. We enter a shallow dive, aimed to bring us about 100ft above the ground at the airfield boundary. Alter

Sqn Ldr Brian Mercer AFC, the Blue Diamonds team leader, in his Hunter with his vintage 1933 Alfa Romeo Gran Sport at Middleton St George in 1961. (Brian Allchin)

◀

The Blue Diamonds diving down for a bomb burst over Cyprus in 1961. (Brian Allchin)

Did you know?

The Black Arrows took their name after a leading French newspaper, describing 'Treble One's' display at Bordeaux on 12 May 1956, had dubbed the team *'les Fleches Volantes'* ('Flying Arrows'). They became accepted universally, courtesy of a French newspaper following the 22nd Paris Salon display of 1 June 1957, as *'les Fleches Noir'*.

course slightly to adjust for wind and maintain our correct approach path. Gently does it; small movements of the lead aircraft require much greater movements by aircraft at the extremities of this large formation. Press the radio button and call our man in the control tower, the squadron adjutant; soon now he will take over Oliver Stewart's task of commentator, a concession not easily extracted from this doyen of Farnborough. Our man tells us that John Cunningham, flying the Comet, is completing his display and we shall be clear to commence on time. And we are on time, to the second.

Below, the compelling voice of Oliver Stewart keeps the attention of the spectators riveted on the Comet on its final approach. They have not spotted us yet, skimming low over the heather of Laffans Plain, even though we are less than a mile

◄◄

The Blue Diamonds
climbing in tight
formation over Cyprus in
1961. (Brian Allchin)

The Blue Diamonds in
line abreast formation.
(Brian Allchin)

➤

The Blue Diamonds looping the loop over Cyprus in 1961. The outside aircraft has still to be painted in blue livery. (Brian Allchin)

away. Gracefully, John Cunningham eases his magnificent aircraft onto the runway; Oliver Stewart reluctantly relinquishes his microphone to our commentator who invites everyone to look now to their left where they will see…! This is it. We are on stage. For the next few minutes the skies above Farnborough are ours; we must make good use of them.

We have about 100 yards to go. We are low. The rearmost aircraft, flying beneath the slipstreams of those in front, is the lowest, 50ft above the ground. But the pilot ignores the ground. He, like all the others, fixes his eyes on the aircraft on which he is formating, concentrating to the exclusion of all else on maintaining his correct position. In every cockpit there is an atmosphere of tense but professional anticipation.

In the lead aircraft I make quick final checks; fuel, enough to complete the display and return to base; airspeed, about 420 knots, good; engine power, 7,200rpm, enough to give 85% power. Don't touch the throttle again now; the others will have enough to do without chasing my throttle movements. Down below the airfield boundary flashes by. Now is the time! Radio a soft warning of intention to the formating pilots and ease firmly, steadily, back on the control column. As one, twenty-two Hunters rise from among the background of the dunes and point skyward.

As we zoom upwards the airspeed falls. Resist the temptation to apply more throttle. We have sufficient speed and inertia to fly over the top of this loop provided we keep the radius correct. Do this by maintaining the right back-pressure on the

Did you know?

From June 1980
to 1994 three RN
two-seat Hunters
converted to T.8M
with FRS.Mk 1 cockpit
instrumentation were
used to acquaint Sea
Harrier pilots under
training with Blue Fox
radar equipment.

control column. Too much or too little and we shall stall; I dismiss from my mind any disturbing thoughts of what could result from twenty-two aircraft stalling in close formation. A glance in the mirror confirms that all aircraft are still in perfect formation. So far, so good. All the Hunters are now standing vertically on their tails. For better or worse we are now virtually committed to completing this loop in some fashion or other. From this altitude there is little one can safely do with so many aircraft, other than loop then. It is the point of no return.

Looking forward along the nose of my aircraft all that can be seen is the clear blue of a cloudless sky; the earth's horizon has disappeared. It is difficult now to keep the path of the loop absolutely perpendicular to the ground, for the limitless sky provides nothing by which direction can be gauged. If the loop is not maintained in the vertical plane then the formation will turn and those aircraft on the inside of the turn must, to stay in position, fly more slowly than those on the outside; perhaps too slowly for comfort. Furthermore, if the loop turns then its position relative to the ground moves laterally, and although started in line with the runway will finish well displaced to one side; perhaps over the crowd; a position not renowned for its popularity with the show organizers, let alone the spectators. But surely we must be nearing the summit now. Throw my head well back and look for the horizon. Ah yes! There it is, and level too; we have kept our flight path vertical and all is well.

As we come to the top of the loop, the halfway point, we encounter a further difficulty. An aircraft flying line astern of another must keep below the jet efflux and slipstream of the one ahead. Consequently, the flight path arcs for aircraft at the rear of the formation are much greater than for those at the front and to maintain station, those at the rear require much more engine power. Unfortunately, at the top of the loop airspeed is low which results in poor thrust response to throttle movements. To keep in formation is difficult; to regain position once it is lost is impossible. But this is not all. As we reach the summit the aircraft in front begin to descend, the speed ceases to fall and we accelerate quite rapidly. This is only true however for the leading aircraft, because those behind have yet to reach the top so they are still decelerating. The result is a tendency for the spacing between aircraft to increase and the shape of the

➤

Flg-Off Brian Allchin in front of J-Juliet of 92 Squadron. (Brian Allchin)

Did you know?

The Swiss operated Hunters for thirty years and the national display team, the Patrouille Suisse, used Hunters from 1970 to 1994 when they re-equipped with the F5E Tiger.

formation to be spoiled. We must prevent this happening.

In effect those of us in front must wait for those following to reach the top of the 'hill'; but if we in front reduce engine power we do not achieve the desired result because the effects of gravity on our acceleration more than compensate for the reduction in thrust. Moreover, the use of air brakes would cause too much air turbulence for precision flying. Fortunately there is another method. We in front delay our downward plunge by holding our aircraft, inverted, nearly level with the horizon by relaxing the back pressure on the control column. Glance again in the mirror. It reveals an impressive sight. As each aircraft in turn tops the 'hill' the sky appears to fill with Hunters each poised, floating, inverted, on the horizon. There is a capriciousness in their attitude, as though they themselves anticipate the exhilarating dive to come as much as the pilots.

Very well then. Here we go. Ease back again on the control column and we swoop rapidly downwards, diving for the runway beneath. The speed builds up giving a renewed crispness to the feel of the controls. If anything the formation packs closer together than before. Mere feet separate wing tip from wing tip. The airfield grows rapidly larger as we hurtle downwards and as the runway becomes near life-size, our impressive formation ceases its downward plunge and sweeps above the airfield no more than a few feet above the ground. One can sense the lightness of spirit and the pride in every cockpit. Perhaps the loop was not immaculate but we know that it was pretty good. One day perhaps another squadron might perform a loop

Did you know?
Instead of adopting the Hunter two-seater to replace the Vampire T.11 the RAF economised by acquiring the Folland Gnat T.2, an aircraft that was not representative of any RAF operational type, could not accommodate the full range of pilots and could not be used for weapons training.

with twenty-two fighter aircraft in close formation and close to the ground and in public but, well, we were the first!

We swing swiftly through to the completion of our demonstration, including a barrel roll with sixteen black Hunters, and then in a matter of moments we are clear of Farnborough and streaking for Odiham. We land and quickly debrief. We are nonchalant. Everything went as planned and practiced, so what is there to talk about? Come on. Pile into our cars and hare over to Farnborough. Rumour has it that there is some free beer somewhere among those marquees with the blue and white-striped awnings.

Twenty-two to one we shall find it!

In 1960 Treble One was selected for the fourth successive year to provide the leading aerobatic team of Fighter Command.

In 1961 and 1962, 92 Squadron's Blue Diamonds' aerobatic team carried on the proud Hunter tradition set by Treble One with the F.6. 'Shiny Blue', commanded by Sqn Ldr Brian Mercer AFC. Often the Blue Diamonds flew three practice shows a day, in addition to their operational flying. The normal repertoire with nine aircraft saw each event being separated by a wing-over or a tight turn in front of the crowd: *Diamond Nine* loop; *Diamond Nine* roll, with smoke; *T-bone* loop, with smoke; *Delta* roll; *Wine-glass* loop (breaking four and five); *Half-Swan* roll, with smoke; *Line-abreast* loop (breaking six and seven); *Box-Five* roll, with smoke; *Bomb-burst* loop, with smoke. After the Hunters had re-formed into two echelons they came in and executed a double loop in echelon. The basic box-four formation readily lends itself to expansion and while initially the team consisted of nine aircraft, it could easily be increased to twelve or sixteen aircraft, allowing in the sixteen-aircraft team four split formations of four aircraft each. 1962 was The Blue Diamonds' last season as a Hunter display team. For the 1963 season the Firebirds of 56 (Lightning) Squadron was selected as the official RAF aerobatic team. Two years later the Red Arrows performed in public for the first time and in 1969 the Reds were established on a permanent basis within the CFS as a squadron in their own right.

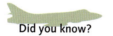

Did you know?

Black Arrows leader Roger Topp had joined the RAF in 1939 and learned to fly in Canada in 1943 before returning to England in 1944, where a surplus of powered aircraft pilots saw him transferred to the Glider Pilot Regiment. On 24 March 1945 he flew a Horsa in the airborne crossing of the Rhine. He chose black, not just because it is part of the traditional Treble One Squadron marking, but because during the Second World War black had changed the whole appearance of the night fighter and made it look a meaner and more impressive aircraft.

In 1960–61, one by one the Hunter squadrons in the UK disbanded and they were largely re-equipped with the English Electric F.1 Lightning supersonic fighter. By April 1961 only five Hunter squadrons remained in Fighter Command and in 1963 the last two Hunter F.6 squadrons began re-equipping with the Lightning F.2, but in 1959 the Hunter had entered one of its most impressive chapters. Hawkers had long been aware of its potential as a very successful ground-attack aircraft and were rewarded when Hunters replaced the de Havilland Venom FB.4 in this role in the Middle East. Seventy-nine Hunter F.6s were modified to full FGA.9 standard and a further fifty-two FGA.9 conversions took place during 1961–65. Each aircraft was fitted with a tail parachute, increased cockpit ventilation and refrigeration, increased pilot's oxygen supply,

and provision for carrying 230-gallon drop tanks. The first FGA.9 (XG135) flew on 3 July 1959, powered by a non-surge Avon 207. Initially, the converted aircraft retained their Avon 203 engines but later most were progressively re-engined with the Avon 207. In addition to the standard four-gun armament, strengthened wings enabled the FGA.9 to carry a wide variety of external stores. The two inboard pylons could carry 500lb or 1,000lb bombs, a cluster of six 3in rocket projectiles, a honeycomb battery containing twenty-four or thirty-seven 2in folding-fin rockets, or a carrier holding two 25lb practice bombs. Removal of the outboard pylons permitted the carrying of four Mk 12 rocket rails each fitted with three 3in rocket projectiles, or four 3in rocket projectiles with 60lb warheads. (In 1967 the 68mm SNEB rocket, which

FGA.9 XG298/E of 43 Squadron at Khormaksar, Aden with camels and security forces. In late 1967 this Hunter was transferred to the Royal Jordanian Air Force. (MoD)

Fred Rawson (right) and Larry Forster load the first of six concrete-headed practice rockets to an 8 Squadron FGA.9 at RAF Khormaksar in the summer of 1963, their last job before returning to the UK. Note the appropriately placed mug of tea - yes tea. Even hot beverages were welcome in the torrid heat of Aden. (Ray Deacon)

8 Squadron FGA.9 XE609 on the Hunter dispersal at Khormaksar in the summer of 1963, depicts the standard configuration implemented on the FGA.9 force for operations in the Middle East; 230-gallon drop tanks on the inner pylons and three rocket rails under each wing. Other identifying features of the Mark 9 include the tail brake chute and lack of gun-blast deflectors. (Ray Deacon)

comprised eighteen rockets in a pod, was fitted to the Hunter's outboard wing pylon to replace the '3in drainpipe' rocket, which dated back to the Second World War.) It brought the Hunter's all-up weight to more than 25,000lb, a remarkable achievement given the hot and high environment that the FGA.9 was to operate in.

Did you know?

The rapidly replaceable gun-pack was lowered from the aircraft on three bomb hoists, the four barrels having been detached and left in the blast-tubes.

When fired, the pack automatically ventilated by opening a small, electronically-operated air-scoop in the starboard gun-bay access panel.

Deliveries to the RAF began in October 1959 when 8 Squadron at Khormaksar, Aden began re-equipping with the type. They were followed in March 1960 by 208 Squadron, which in June 1960 flew to Nairobi, Kenya and began operating from Eastleigh. On 25 June the Iraqi Prime Minister, General Abdul Karim Kassim, announced that neighbouring Kuwait was an integral part of his country. Under an existing agreement Britain prepared to send military assistance to the small Arab kingdom, especially since Iraq might be expected to attack Kuwait around 14 July (the Iraqi National Day). On 30 June 1961 the FGA.9s were flown to Bahrain to meet the anticipated threat. Ironically Iraq at this time included two squadrons of Hunter F.6s in its inventory. In the first week of July, the RAF Hunters landed at Kuwait's new airport. However, the Iraqi threat to Kuwait did not materialize and eventually the FGA.9s returned to Khormaksar and Bahrain.

As Kenya was to gain independence from Britain, 208 Squadron moved to Aden during 1962. President Abdul Nasser of Egypt attempted to remove the British from Aden using armed insurgents in the neighbouring state of Yemen. A mountainous area known as the Radfan, twenty miles long by fifteen miles wide, thirty-five miles north of Aden, was the main stronghold of the Yemeni-backed insurgents. The Hunter FGA.9s and a few Shackletons carried out leaflet-dropping missions, followed by bombing strikes against the insurgents in the Radfan. On 1 March 1963, 43 Squadron, which had converted to the FGA.9 in Cyprus, moved to Khormaksar. During early 1964

A line-up of FGA.9s on the Kuwait new apron in July 1961 during the first Gulf Crisis comprising 8 Squadron's XF376/Q, with a 208 Squadron 'zap' on the forward fuselage and seven 208 Squadron aircraft. (The Aviation Bookshop, via Ray Deacon)

an increased number of hit and run raids by Yemeni aircraft on villages close to the Aden border culminated in an attack by an armed helicopter and two MiG fighters on a village and a frontier guard post. The RAF was ordered to attack Yemeni insurgents who had gained control of a fort at Harib. Hunters dropped leaflets to warn the civilian population before beginning their attack on 28 March, which was followed

An 8 Squadron FGA.9 is given the all-clear to taxi out by Pete Wotton at Khormaksar in the autumn of 1963. Pete is dressed appropriately for working on the hot concrete pan, a sweat-towel ready to mop his brow. (Ray Deacon)

under cover of darkness by a parachute drop by 22 SAS.

At daybreak on the 29th the SAS came under heavy fire and before long they were surrounded by three times the expected numbers of enemy tribesmen, armed with mortars and machine-guns. Eighteen Hunter sorties were flown and 127 3in rockets and over 7,000 rounds of 30mm cannon were fired on the rebels.

Former Black Arrow F.6 XF446 was converted to FGA.9 standard for the RAF in 1965 and issued to 54 Squadron, in whose markings it is seen. The aircraft was later converted to F.56A configuration and delivered to India. 54 Squadron operated Hunters from 1955 to 1969. (Ray Deacon collection)

The battle raged for thirty hours and two British troopers were killed. British ground forces supported by the FGA.9s later harried and hunted down the rebels. Non-stop attacks were made during May and into June, 43 Squadron alone flying more than 150 sorties and firing 1,000 rockets and 50,000 rounds of ammunition. On 18 November 1964, following a series of rocket and cannon strafing attacks by the

Sharjah is the location of this 43 Squadron FGA.9 while the squadron was on a short detachment. (The Aviation Bookshop, via Ray Deacon)

Did you know?

It is rumoured that a C-130 of the 36th TAS, USAF that was taken aloft by a disaffected ground-crewman at Mildenhall on 23 May 1969, was shot down in the English Channel near Alderney by a RAF Hunter, which was sent to intercept the errant Hercules.

Hunters, the last remaining dissident tribe capitulated. Fighting continued in Aden and the Hunters were used until Britain withdrew in 1967. 43 Squadron flew its last ground-attack sorties on 9 November before being disbanded as a Hunter squadron. Hunters of Nos 8 and 208 Squadrons which formed the Offensive Support Wing at Muharraq, Bahrain remained until 1971 when both Hunter squadrons were disbanded.

British forces based in Singapore and Malaysia as part of the South East Asia Treaty Organisation (SEATO) included sixteen FGA.9s of 20 Squadron at Tengah, Singapore which provided Day Fighter/Ground Attack for the whole theatre, and four FGA.9s of 28 Squadron at Kai Tak in Hong Kong. Indonesia had a policy of 'confrontation' (not all-out war) against the new Malaysian Federation and the SEATO air component was responsible for countering Indonesian Air Force incursions. Although the IAF comprised mostly obsolete F-51 Mustangs and B-25 Mitchell bombers, it was equipped with a number of Soviet fighter and bomber aircraft. (A Hunter and a MiG-17 actually chased each other around the sky on one occasion, although no shots were fired.) In September 1963 a greater RAF and RAAF presence ensued when Indonesian-backed guerrillas began infiltrating Malaysian territory. Indonesian propaganda flights over North Borneo increased and on 20 February 1964, four Hunter FGA.9s of 20 Squadron each detached to Labuan and Kuching flying surveillance and CAP in the ADIZ (Air Defence Identification Zone) encompassing North Borneo and Sarawak.

71

72

◀◀
208 Squadron FGA.9 on the Khormaksar Hunter pan in March 1964. 208 Squadron operated Hunters from 1960 to 1971. (Ray Deacon)

◀
FGA.9 XK137/D of 45 'Flying Camels' Squadron airborne from Wittering in December 1972. (Via Group Captain Hastings)

In August-September Indonesian paratroops landed in force in Western Malaysia and the FGA.9s, each armed with sixteen 3in RPs fitted with semi-armour-piercing warheads, flew rocket- and cannon-firing strikes. Results were unknown as 1km squares of jungle were attacked with no particular targets in sight but by the end of September almost all the Indonesian troops had either been killed or captured. Thereafter, Indonesian incursions in Malaysia were smaller and more sporadic.

➤

FGA.9s of 45 Squadron on a sortie from Wittering in December 1972. The famous 'Flying Camel' emblem had been adopted fifty years earlier. (Via Group Captain Hastings)

FGA.9s operating from Tengah carried out rocket strikes and strafing attacks on guerilla concentrations in the Malay peninsular. Some Indonesian troops landed east of Changi on the night of 30 May 1965 and quickly gained a foothold in an old Second World War Japanese fortification to await further reinforcements. Four FGA.9s directed by a FAC (Forward Air Controller), made rocket- and cannon-strafing attacks to dislodge them. Thirteen infiltrators were captured and the rest captured or killed later. On 1 September two B-25 Mitchells were strafed. When a Whirlwind helicopter was shot down, four extra Hunters were sent to Sarawak. From October 1965 RAAF Sabres started to take over border patrol and escort duty from the Hunters. The unofficial war largely fizzled out and the confrontation finally ended on 11 August 1966. Late in December, 28 Squadron disbanded while 20 Squadron remained at RAF Tengah until February 1970.

In Britain in early 1961 Nos 1 and 54 Squadrons which were equipped with FGA.9s formed the RAF contribution to the Allied Command Europe Mobile Forces, dedicated to the rapid reinforcement of the NATO flanks. Yet early in 1963, 54 Squadron FGA.9s carried out border patrol duties along the Yemen border until relieved by 43 Squadron's FGA.9s. In August 1 and 54 Squadrons moved to West Raynham, Norfolk where they participated in air defence and reinforcement exercises in the Mediterranean and West Germany. When General Franco applied political pressure against Gibraltar, they increased the RAF presence at the Rock with three- and four-week detachments. The formation of RAF

FGA.9, XJ695/Q of
58 Squadron just after
take-off from Wittering
in September 1973.
(Richard Wilson)

Did you know?

The Hunter was armed
with four electrically
fired and controlled
30mm Aden cannon
with 150 rounds
per gun, but it was
found that the feed
operated more reliably
if the ammunition
was restricted to
135 rounds per gun,
which corresponded
to just less than seven
seconds' fire.

Strike Command on 30 April 1968 left the two NATO mobile FGA.9 squadrons as the tactical support and strike force. In July 1969 1 Squadron left for Wittering to begin conversion to the Harrier and 54 Squadron was disbanded on 1 September.

At the end of 1971 the last FGA.9s were finally withdrawn from first-line service when 8 Squadron returned to the UK from the Gulf to disband. In June 1972 it was announced that two fully operational DF/GA (Day Fighter/Ground Attack) squadrons equipped with Hunters would be formed to train the new generation of fighter pilots for the Phantom, Lightning and Harrier squadrons. After September 1974 a dedicated training school, the Tactical Weapons Unit (TWU) was established at RAF Brawdy, Pembrokeshire and on 26 July 1976, Nos 45 and 58 Squadrons were disbanded. At its peak, TWU operated about seventy Hunters in four 'shadow squadrons', which, in time of crisis, would have become first-line squadrons. In 1978 the TWU was split into two. Brawdy became a Hawk station. All the Hunters moved to 2 TWU at Lossiemouth, Scotland and in 1980 it too changed to Hawks.

The last Hunters in RAF service were the ex-RAF and FAA two-seaters of 237 OCU at Honington, Suffolk which had been established in 1971 to provide dual-control facilities for RAF pilots who were to convert to the HS Buccaneer S.2. The two-seat Hunters provided an Integrated Flight Instrumentation System (IFIS) as a link between the Hawk advanced trainer and the operational Buccaneers at RAF Honington. The last operational RAF T.Mk 7s were withdrawn from use with 237

◄◄

Sqn Ldr Callum Kerr in FGA.9 XG261/64 ripples off a SNEB pod at the Theddlethorpe Range in June 1974. On 29 June 1976 the Flying Camels disbanded. (MoD)

◄

Having participated in the 1958 Venom Replacement Evaluation Trials alongside the Gnat F.1 and Jet Provost T.3, XK150 was converted to FGA.9 standard and issued to 8 Squadron at Khormaksar in 1960. This photograph was taken during a squadron detachment to Rhodesia later in the year. Following the British withdrawal from Aden in 1967, XK150 was presented to the RJAF. (Ray Deacon collection)

OCU in March 1994. In December the T.Mk 8s and GA.Mk 11s from FRADU at Yeovilton followed them. Many were obtained by individuals and organisations in the UK, and even in countries where the aircraft never operated such as the USA, Brazil, New Zealand and South Africa.

In May 1954 negotiations with Fokker of Holland and Avions Fairey and SABCA of Belgium for the manufacture of the Hunter in those countries were completed with funding for the manufacture of the Hunters provided by the USA. Dutch-built Hunter 4s started coming off the Fokker production line before the end of 1955 and began equipping the Koninklijke Luchtmacht. Twenty Hunter trainers were also ordered that same year. In 1957 manufacture of F.6s began. These were modified to carry Sidewinder missiles on outboard wing stations. In Belgium Hunter F.4s served with Force Aerienne Belge/ Belgische Luchtmacht front-line units for about ten years. In 1958 these began to be replaced by licence-built Mk 6s which remained in service until replacement by the Lockheed F-104 Starfighter in the early

1960s. Total licence production was ninety-six Dutch F.4s and 93 F.6s, 111 Belgian F.4s and 144 F.6s.

In Scandinavia on 29 June 1954, Sweden signed an order for 120 Hunter Mk 50s for the Flygvapnet. Denmark signed a contract for thirty F.4s (Mk 51s) on 3 July 1954.

Both the Danish and Swedish Hunters were not fitted with wing-leading edge extensions. The first Swedish Hunter Mk 50 made its maiden flight on 24 June 1955 and production continued until 1958. The first Mk 51 was flown on 15 December 1955 and all deliveries to the Kongelige

Duncan Simpson, Hawker test pilot 1954–78, in the cockpit of G-BABM, which was acquired by Singapore. It displays the flags of eighteen countries that bought the Hunter. (Duncan Simpson)

Hawker Hunter of the Peruvian Air Force. (Duncan Simpson)

➤

FGA.70A of the Lebanese Air Force in the 1970s. On 17 November 2008 three Hunters were once more fully operational with the LAF at Rayak Airbase! Other surviving Hunters in storage are thought to include L-282 (pictured). The LAF ordered its first Hunters in 1958 and by around 1994 the last LAF Hunters had been retired.

Dansk Flyvevâben were made in 1956. The Swedish Hunters – designated the J 34 and converted to carry Sidewinder air-to-air missiles – remained in front-line service until 1966, flying with four Wings. In Danish service ESK 724 was disbanded on 31 March 1974 and most of the nineteen surviving Hunters including two T.Mk 53 trainers delivered in late 1958 were repurchased and presented to museums in Britain.

When Hunters were withdrawn in the Belgian Air Force from 1962 and in 1963 the Mk 6 was declared redundant in the

RNAF, many had seldom exceeded 600 airframe hours and Hawkers subsequently refurbished them for sale to overseas customers in South America, Africa and the Middle and Far East. Kuwait for instance, received nine ex-Belgian, Dutch and RAF Mk 6s in 1965–66. The single-seaters were withdrawn from service late in 1976 but the five T.Mk 67 (all with Avon 200-series engines) two-seaters continued in the training role for some time. Sixteen ex-RAF F.4s acquired by Peru and known as the Hunter Mk 52 were delivered by sea in April 1956 and they entered service with

Iraqi Air Force FGA.59 taxiing in after a final test flight at Dunsfold shortly before departing for Iraq in 1964. It was converted from a former Belgian-built F.6 dating from 1957. (HSA)

Hunter FGA.57 of the
Kuwait Air Force. (BAe)

Did you know?

Of the 1,972 Hunters
manufactured in the
UK and in Holland
and Belgium, 526
aircraft were returned
to Hawker Siddeley
Aircraft and rebuilt to
as new condition to
fulfil new orders.

the Fuerza Aerea Peruana before the end of the year. In 1959 a two-seat Hunter was acquired and became the Hunter Mk 62, entering service in March 1960. Eleven of the Peruvian Hunters were still in service in the late 1970s. During 1966–88 Chile received fifteen single-seat, ex-RAF, Dutch and Belgian Hunters as FGA.Mk 71s. By September 1973 thirteen more FGA.71s, six single-seat fighter-reconnaissance Mk 71As and six two-seater T.Mk 72s were also received. In 1974 an embargo on the

Hunter of the Swedish Air
Force.

Did you know?
India was the third
largest user of the
Hunter after the UK
and Belgium with 252
Hunters. The Belgian
Air Force operated 256
Hunters manufactured
by Fokker in Holland
and assembled in
Belgium.

During 1974 and 1975
Kenya became the last
customer for refurbished
Hunters when it acquired
four ex-RAF single-seat
FGA.Mk 80s and two
ex- Fleet Air Arm T. Mk
81s. (BAe)

Swiss Air Force Hunters
hangared in huge caves
cut into the Alps. (Swiss
Air Force)

supply of spares to Chile was imposed and by 1978 only twenty aircraft remained serviceable. After twenty-eight years the Hunter was finally retired from service on 17 February 1995.

In 1963 Rhodesia (now Zimbabwe) ordered a dozen Hunter FGA.9s and these ex-RAF Mk 6s equipped No.1 Squadron of the Royal Rhodesian Air Force. The government of Ian Smith made a Unilateral

Declaration of Independence (UDI) in November 1965 and the resulting trade embargo made servicing difficult without the influx of spares. Even so, nine of the original dozen Hunters were still flying with the Zimbabwe-Rhodesian Air Force at the end of the 1970s and a four-man formation aerobatic team gave displays in the late 1960s and early '70s. Late in 1972 a major insurgency broke out and the Rhodesian Air Force operated against the Patriotic Front for seven years. During the war against the insurgents only two of the Hunters were shot down.

During the late 1960s and early 1970s the small oil states and Emirates of Abu Dhabi, Qatar and Oman also received Hunters with training often supervised by RAF personnel. The Abu Dhabi Air Force was formed at Sharjah with seven

◄◄
*Swiss Air Force Hunters.
(Swiss Air Force)*

◄
*Swiss Air Force
F.58A, J-4105 and
F.58, J-4007, practise
synchronised raising of
their undercarriages as
they depart Dübendorf
Airbase in 1981. Both are
currently preserved, J-
4007 in Interlaken and J-
4105, a conversion from
ex-RAF F.4, XF303, in the
USA. (Urs Harnisch, via
Ray Deacon)*

Hunter FGA.Mk 76s and three FR.Mk 76As converted from RAF aircraft. Two T.Mk 77s converted from Dutch T.Mk 7s were delivered during 1970 and 1971. In 1975 Sultan Qaboos presented them to King Hussein of Jordan to help in making good his losses sustained in the Yom Kippur War of 1973. Two Hunter FGA.Mk 78s and one

◄◄
Extensive lines of Hawker Hunters in pristine condition were common at many Swiss military airfields across the country for thirty-six years from the late '50s through to the early '90s. This scene was captured at Ambri Airbase in April 1985 and depicts F.58s of 3 Squadron. (Unknown, via Ray Deacon)

◄
Two Swiss Air Force F.58s about to land in formation in 1988. (Urs Harnisch)

T.Mk 79 were delivered for service in the Qatar Public Safety Forces in December 1971 and these were followed later by a further four refurbished aircraft. In 1975 the Sultan of Oman's Air Force received from Jordan about thirty-one Hunters collected from various sources. These were used in operations in the Dhofar and

➤

*The Wildstrubel
Mountains provide the
stunning backdrop for
this Swiss Air Force T.68,
J-4205 as it climbs over
the snow-clad peaks
below. Rebuilt in 1975
from a Swedish single-
seat F.51 dating from
1957, J-4205 was retired
in 1994 into the hands
of the Flieger Museum
Altenrhein and is
maintained in airworthy
condition for the display
circuit and passenger
flights. (Urs Harnisch, via
Ray Deacon)*

were flown by mercenary pilots on cross-border operations armed with Pakistani 1,025lb bombs and 88mm Hispano SURA rockets and 30mm Aden for strafing. In 1979 twelve Hunters were serving with the Sultan's No.6 Squadron at Thumrait, his Air Force's principal strike base. The remaining aircraft were retained in storage as replacements and to provide spares for the operational aircraft.

During 1970–71 sixteen refurbished ex-RAF Hunter 6s were acquired by The Republic of Singapore as FGA.Mk 74s and FR.Mk 74As. Based at Tengah, they were

Swiss Hunter on finals at Dübendorf in August 1990. (Author)

Did you know?
It was with the F.5 in the 1956 Suez Campaign that the Hunter first saw active service when, although none were tested in combat, two were destroyed on the ground in Cyprus by terrorists.

used for air defence, army support and tactical reconnaissance, armed with SNEB-Matra rockets. By October 1973 twenty-two Mk 74B single-seaters and nine T 75As and 75Bs 4s had joined them. During 1974 and 1975 Kenya became the last customer for refurbished Hunters when it acquired four ex-RAF single-seat FGA.Mk 80s and two ex-Fleet Air Arm T. Mk 81s.

In 1957 India had ordered twenty-two new-build Hunter T 66s, which were delivered by the end of 1960. These resulted from a request in November 1954 by India for Hawkers to outline specification, costs

Swiss Hunters at
Dübendorf in August
1990. (Author)

Hunters in service. After the Indo-Pakistani war of September 1965, India ordered fifty-three Hunter Mk 56A aircraft. At the beginning of the second Indo-Pakistani conflict of 3–17 December 1971, India had a force of 127 single-seat Hunters and twenty-eight two-seaters. The conflict cost India twenty-two Hunters. By 1979 eighty Hunters remained in front-line service with four Strike Squadrons of the Indian Air Force and about twenty older Marks were employed on target-towing duties and another twenty-three aircraft served the OCU. In 1996 the Hunter was retired from front-line service when the Thunderbolts' display team received replacement aircraft.

and delivery dates for 100 Hunter aircraft. In April 1956 India evaluated the Hunter 4 and 6 in the air and on the ground and in July 1957 agreed to purchase 160 Hunter F.6 aircraft (designated Mk 56). By the end of 1960 the entire order, which included sixteen refurbished RAF aircraft, equipped five squadrons of the Indian Air Force. Flying accidents during the first four years of service reduced the number of

In 1958 Switzerland ordered 100 Hunter Mk 6s for the Flugwaffe after comparative evaluation trials involving the F-86D, T-33 Shooting Star, Mystere IV, P-16 and Gnat.

The first twelve Swiss Hunter Mk 58s were all ex-RAF Mk 6s and the last of the contract were delivered by April 1960. The Swiss Hunters were adapted to carry Sidewinder missiles for the air interception role. In 1969 Switzerland ordered thirty Mk 58A single-seaters for delivery during 1971–73 and twenty-two more followed during January 1974 to April 1975. In addition, eighty-two two-seat T.Mk 68s were ordered.

The Flugwaffe finally retired the last of its Hunters on 16 December 1994.

In the Middle East in 1957–58, Iraq received sixteen ex-RAF Hunter 6s but the revolution curtailed any further orders for some time. In 1958–59 Lebanon and The Air Force of the Hashemite Kingdom of Jordan each received six ex-RAF Hunter 6s. Lebanon later received three T.Mk 66Cs and four FGA.Mk 70s, all converted from

A pair of Swiss Hunters landing at Dübendorf in August 1990. (Author)

Swiss Hunters taxi out at Dübendorf in August 1990. (Author)

Swiss Hunter at Dübendorf in August 1990. (Author)

Changing a gun pack on a Swiss Hunter. (Author)

Belgian Mk 6s. Of these, five were lost in training accidents and six more Mk 70s were ordered in 1975 from RAF stocks. Early in 1963 Iraq ordered twenty-four ground-attack Hunter Mk 59s, which were converted from the Belgian aircraft to FGA. Mk 9 standard. In 1965 and 1966 these were followed by twenty-two more Mk 59/B aircraft and fifty-two two-seaters converted from Belgian single-seaters. At the beginning of the 'Six-Day War' against Israel in 1967 the Iraqi Air Force had on strength sixty-four single-seat Hunters and four two-seaters. In Jordan the entire strength of the JAF's No.1 Squadron, including a number of Hunter FGA.9s was destroyed by the Israeli Air Force's heavy strike attack on Mafraq. Only two Hunters survived the attack and these were badly damaged. These losses were offset by

Several Hunters received special colour schemes towards the end of the type's service with the Swiss Air Force. One of these, 7 Squadron F.58, J-4007, bore attractive blue and yellow squadron colours for three days during 1989 and was photographed at Payerne Airbase with a Maverick missile on the outer pylon. It is currently preserved by the Hunter Verein Interlaken. (Ray Deacon collection)

the presentation of three single-seaters by Saudi Arabia. In June 1972 the Hunters on strength with the JAF amounted to thirty-five single-seaters and three two-seaters. These aircraft were scheduled for replacement when in October 1973 the Yom Kippur War began. Iraq possessed forty-eight Hunters which joined Syrian MiG-2s in flying top-cover over the Northern Front while Sukhoi Su-7s carried out their ground-attack strikes. The Iraqi Hunter pilots tended to avoid combat with Israeli Phantoms but frequently engaged A-4 Skyhawks and Super Mystères. Seven Iraqi Hunters were lost during this war but they claimed about twelve Israeli aircraft destroyed between 12–24 October. In 1975 Abu Dhabi presented to King Hussein their entire strength of twelve Hunters to join the nineteen surviving Jordanian

➤
F.58, J-4040 with flaps down and air brake extended over the Wildstrubel Mountains. Shortly before the disbandment of 15 Squadron in 1993, the Squadron Commander, Ueli Leutert, decided to have J-4040 repainted in a scheme representing the unit emblem, a paper aeroplane. The new all-white livery was adorned with the 'Fliegerstaffel 15' logo, the names of squadron pilots and groundcrew on the wings and spine. (Urs Harnisch, via Ray Deacon)

aircraft. Later that same year King Hussein presented all his Hunters to the Sultan of Oman. By 1979 Iraq was still flying at least thirty Hunters.

As part of the so-called 'Magic Carpet' arms deal with Saudi Arabia, Hawker was contracted to supply the Royal Saudi Air Force with four Hunter Mk 6s and two

Another view of J-4040 flying over the snow-capped Wildstrubel Mountains. Commonly known by its nickname, Papyrus, J-4040 is preserved in airworthy condition by the Hunter Verein Obersimmental at its former base, St Stephan, and is a regular performer at air shows across Europe. (Urs Harnisch, via Ray Deacon)

Mk 7s early in 1966. The Hunters reached Riyadh in May 1966 and they were used to form 6 Squadron RSAF at Khamis Mushayt. When Egyptian Air Force MiG-21s and I1-28s carried out a number of attacks on Saudi Arabia, the Hunters were unable to intercept any of the raiders owing to an almost total lack of ground control and

Did you know?
Following Independence in 1980, Zimbabwe obtained four FGA.80s and one T.81 from Kenya. A number of Hunters were destroyed by a guerrilla attack on Thornhill Airbase on 25 July 1982.

their pilots were used instead on retaliatory ground strikes. Though the orders received from the Middle East for Hunters were small, they paved the way for the massive British arms deals for aircraft such as the Lightning, Hawk and the Tornado. All the refurbishment activity helped fund other projects, not least of which was the highly successful P.1127/Kestrel/Harrier series.

◄◄

◄▼

Swiss Air Force Patrouille de Suisse display team taking off from Greenham Common, (Author)

▼

Line-up of Swiss Air Force Patrouille de Suisse display team. (Author)

Swiss Air Force Patrouille de Suisse display team taking off. (Author)

AZF1258 flying high over the Zimbabwe hinterland in 1997. Built in 1956 as an F.6 for the RAF, it saw little service and was one of twelve converted to FGA.9 standard and delivered to Rhodesia in 1963. (Ian Malcolm, via Ray Deacon)

RSAF 528 began life as F.4, XF970 with the RAF in 1956 and saw service with several squadrons until being placed in storage in the early '60s. In 1971 the aircraft was converted to T.75A standard with the more powerful 207-series Avon and delivered to Singapore in 1972. Retired in 1994, 528 was purchased by former Rhodesian Air Force pilot Dave Currie a year later and restored to airworthy condition at Archerfield Airport in Brisbane, Australia. (Ray Deacon collection)

Number 853 was a former Jordanian Hunter FGA.73 donated to the SOAF in 1975. It was built originally as an F.6 in 1956 and it saw little service with the RAF before conversion to FR.10 standard in 1961. It was subsequently modified to Jordanian standards and delivered in 1971. Upon withdrawal, this splendid aircraft was fully restored for static display and presented to the RAF Museum at Hendon, where it is currently on display. (Ray Deacon collection)

At first glance this may appear to be Jordanian FGA.73A J-708, but it is in fact Indian Air Force F.56A, A471 painted in RJAF markings for the 1966 Farnborough Air Show. Built in 1958 by Avions Fairey in Brussels as an F.6 for the Belgian Air Force, it was withdrawn five years later. (Ray Deacon)

➤

Bearing the striking blue and white colours of the 'Thunderbirds' display team of the Indian Air Force is F.56A, BA312A. (IAF, via Ray Deacon)

➤

Six Indian Air Force Hunters of No.2 Target Tug Flight at Kalaikunda Airbase in 1999. It disbanded in November 2001. (The Aviation Bookshop, via Ray Deacon)

J-734 is an FR.71A of the Chilean Air Force and is currently one of several Hunters preserved in Santiago. (Ray Deacon collection)

The once prominent features and Patrouille de Suisse colour scheme of former Swiss Air Force F.58, J-4025 were removed before it was restored in Jordanian Air Force markings for presentation to the Royal Jordanian Historic Flight. Here, it touches down at Kemble after participation at a UK air show in 1997, shortly before its ferry flight to Amman. (Glen Moreman)

First flown as an F.4 for the RAF in 1955, XE685 was converted to GA.11 for the Royal Navy in 1963 for air warfare instructor training and conversion flights. Bearing the markings of FRADU, it was a regular participant in the 'Thursday War', in which GA.11s simulated missiles being fired from aircraft attacking ships at sea. (HSA)

Affectionately known as 'gappux', T.66A, G-APUX was built from the rear end and wings from a pair of damaged Belgian F.6s and the front section from a static display unit. First flown as the Hawker demonstrator in 1959, 'gappux' went on to give countless demonstrations to would-be purchasers all over the world. From 1963 it spent periods on loan to the Iraqi, Lebanese and Jordanian Air Forces for pilot training, before being converted to T.72 specification and resale to the Chilean Air Force in 1967. It is currently displayed at the National Aviation Museum. (Peter Amos, via Ray Deacon)

Currently preserved in flying condition with Skyblue Aviation Ltd at North Weald, T.7, XL600 was involved in a bizarre incident in 1963 when, during a slow roll, the second pilot was ejected through the canopy and killed due to his seat not being locked into position. Still in its former 4 FTS colour scheme, it was photographed on the pan at Laarbruch in 1981 when assigned to the airfield's Station Flight. (The Aviation Bookshop, via Ray Deacon)

With high attrition rates being experienced on the Gnat at Valley in the late '60s and with Gnat production having ceased, the decision was taken to fill the void with Hunter Marks 6 and 7. They entered service in camouflage (F.6) and grey with red stripes (T.7) in 1967 but received this attractive red and white colour scheme a few years later, coincident with the plating over of the gun ports. XG274-71 is a fine example of a 4 FTS Hunter of the period and is seen on the pan at Valley in the early '70s. (HSA)

➤
After a long service with the Swiss Air Force, F.58, J-4066 was donated for preservation and was one of a number of Hunters purchased by Mark Hanna for the Old Flying Machine Company in 1998. With brake chute deployed, Mark is about to land the Hunter at Kemble for short-term storage with Delta Jets. J-4066 is currently one of two being operated on contract out of Bournemouth by its new owner, Hunter Aviation at Scampton. (Glen Moreman)

➤
Hunter N72602 of Flight Systems at Mojave Airport, California in 1987. The livery is 54 Squadron RAF. (Author)

Mark Hanna taxiing F.58A, XF303 of the Old Flying Machine Company out at Duxford in the 1990s. This Hunter flew with the Swiss Air Force. (Author)

Former Swiss Air Force F.Mk 58, J-4089 now owned and flown by the Scandinavian Flight. This Hunter first flew on 8 December 1959. (Author)

After fourteen years service with the RAF, XJ689 was converted to FR.74A standard for the RSAF and delivered in 1971. It continued in service until 1992 and is currently based at Momona in New Zealand where it is seen here in 2001. (David Phillips)

T.Mk 7, XL577 in beautiful Blue Diamonds livery at Kemble on 23 June 2007. (Author)

With fare-paying passengers on board, T.68s, J-4205 and J-4201 complete their display to the crowds at the 2008 Hunterfest at St Stephan. (Ray Deacon)

T.68s, J-4205 and J-4201 at the 2008 Hunterfest at St Stephan. (Ray Deacon)

F.Mk 58A, J-4104 built as F.Mk 4, XF947 in 1956 is owned and flown by Jonathon Whaley, owner of Heritage Aviation Developments Ltd. (Author)

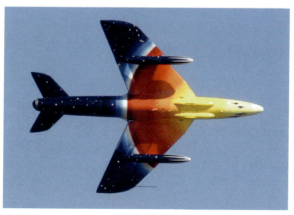

This beautiful aircraft is called Miss Demeanour *and has Jonathon Whaley's family star signs on the rear fuselage, tailfin and wingtips and even the drop tanks look like stars when viewed from the front. (Author)*

Did you know?

On the second day of the Indo-Pakistani war on 7 September 1965, five Indian Air Force Hunters from one formation were shot down in as many minutes by a Pakistani F-86F-40 Sabre flown by Sqn Ldr Mohammed Alam of the Pakistani Air Force. Caught by surprise, the first Hunter was shot down by a Sidewinder missile and the rest by gunfire.

SPECIFICATIONS

Dimensions

Wing Span (all Mks) 33ft 8in (10.25m); Overall Length (all single-seat, except Mk 10 (45ft 10½ in (13.98m); (Mk 10) 46ft 1in (14.02m); (all two-seat) 48ft 10½in (14.89m); Overall Height (all Mks) 13ft 2in (4.0m); Wing Area (all Mks, without leading-edge extensions) 340sq ft (31.62sq in); (all Mks, with leading-edge extensions) 349sq ft (32.42sq m)

Weights (Empty)

(Mk 1) 12,128lb (5,501kg); (Mk 6, 56, 58, 59, 66B & 70) 12,760lb (5,788kg); (T.7, 8, 53 & 62) 13,360lb (6,060kg); (FGA.9) 13,010lb (5,901kg)

Power plants

(Mk 1, 4, T.7, 8, 50, 52, 53 & 62) One 7,200lb/7,425lb (3,265kg/3,367kg) s.t Rolls-Royce Avon Mk 100 series engine; (Mk 6, FGA.9, 10, 12, 56, 58, 59A, 66, 70 & 73) One 10,000lb (4,536kg) s.t. Rolls-Royce Avon 200 series engine; (Mk 2 & 5) One 8,000lb (3,629kg) s.t. Armstrong-Siddeley Sapphire Mk 101

Performance **(Rolls-Royce Avon)**	(Single-seat): max speed: Mach 0.93–Mach 0.95 at 36,000ft (10,973m); 699mph–714mph asl. Service ceiling: 48,800ft (14,874m)–51,000ft (15,697m)
	(Two-seater): max speed: Mach 0.92–Mach 0.93 at 36,000ft (10,973m), 693mph–699mph asl. Service ceiling: 47,000ft (14,905m)–48,900ft (14,326m)
Performance **(Sapphire 101)**	Max speed: Mach 0.94 at 36,000ft (10,973m), 703mph asl; service ceiling: 50,000ft (15,240m)
Armament	(Single-seat) Four 30mm Aden cannon with 150rpg maximum. (Mk 1 & 2: No provision for underwing stores.) Two underwing 1,000lb (454kg) free-fall bombs or two 100-gallon (455-litre) Napalm tanks; (Mk 6 onwards). Two additional underwing pylons capable of carrying 100-gallon (455-litre) Napalm tanks or 52mm honeycomb rocket projectile packs or twelve 3m (78mm) rocket projectiles or four 3m (76mm) 60lb (27.2kg) head rocket projectiles or combinations of 5in (130mm) HVAR, Oerlikon, Bofors and Hispano rocket projectiles of various sizes. (Single-seat

Did you know?
In Swiss service Hunters were fitted with a brake parachute for operation from the country's smaller mountain airfields and starting in 1982 provision for operating with the Hughes AGM-65B Maverick air-to-ground guided missile was made.

Mk 11 and T.8) Adapted for FAA to carry two Martin AGM-12B Bullpup AAMs. Export versions (ground attack role): Sidewinder AAMs, ALQ-171 jammer pods and two 1,000lb (454kg) free-fall bombs on fuselage centre-line

(Two-seat) One 30mm Aden cannon. (Mk 66) Two 30mm Aden cannon

Did you know?

In March 1967 when the 61,000-ton super-tanker *Torrey Canyon* crashed into the Seven Stones reef off Land's End, broke into three pieces and began leaking her entire cargo of 118,000 tons of crude oil, Royal Navy Buccaneer S.2s dropped bombs and relays of Hunters dropped 100-gallon tanks containing kerosene to stoke up the blaze, but the oil refused to burn. Hunter FGA.9s also dropped 100-gallon drop-tanks filled with Napalm and fired 3in rockets into the *Torrey Canyon* but they were unsuccessful and air operations were suspended.

MILESTONES

1947 2 September: First flight of the P.1040 prototype.

1951 1 July: WB188 prototype has first engine run.

1951 20 July: First flight of the WB188 prototype.

1952 5 May: First flight of WB195, the second P.1067.

1952 6 September: Public debut of the Hunter, at Farnborough.

16 May: First flight of WT555, the first production Hunter F.1.

1953 19 September: Neville Duke and WB188 set a new 100km closed circuit world record at 709.2mph.

1954 23 January: First flight of the P.1099 prototype (XF833).

1954 May: Negotiations by Fokker of Holland and Avions Fairey and SABCA of Belgium to manufacture Hunters completed.

1954 29 June: Sweden signs an order for 120 Hunter Mk 50s for the Flygvapnet.

1954 July: Hunter F.1 issued to the CFE and to 43 Squadron at RAF Leuchars, Scotland. Denmark signs contract for thirty Hunter Mk 4s.

1954 19 October: First flight of the F.5.

1954 20 October: First flight of the F.4.

1954 November: India submits a request for Hawkers to outline specification, costs and delivery dates for 100 Hunters.

1955 8 July: First flight of the P.1101 trainer prototype (XJ615).

1955 25 March: First flight of the first F.6 (WW592).

1955: Hunter F.4 issued to thirteen squadrons in 2nd Tactical Air Force (2nd TAF) in Germany.

1956 2 November: Hunters fly top cover sorties in support of naval fighter-bombers during Operation *Musketeer*, the **1956 November** Anglo-French occupation of the Suez Canal zone in Egypt.

1956 November: Seven fighter squadrons are equipped with the Hunter F.4 in the UK and thirteen in 2nd Tactical Air Force.

1956 November: First Hunter F.6s begin re-equipping four squadrons in the UK and seven more follow in 1957.

1957: July India agrees to purchase 160 Hunter F.6 aircraft.

1957 July: Nine of the thirteen Hunter F.4 squadrons in 2nd TAF disbanded. All Hunter squadrons in Fighter Command and the five F.4 Squadrons in Germany complete re-equipment with Hunter F.6s. T.7s enter RAF service.

1958 1 September: Treble One Squadron's Black Arrows perform Twenty-Two Hunter loop at Farnborough.

1958: Switzerland orders 100 Hunter Mk 6s for the Flugwaffe.

1959 3 July: First flight of the FGA.9 (XG135).

1959 October: Delivery of the FGA.9 to the RAF begins.

1960: Treble One selected for the fourth successive year to provide the leading aerobatic team of Fighter Command.

1961–1962: 92 Squadron's Blue Diamonds' provide the leading aerobatic team of Fighter Command.

1961 April: Only five Hunter squadrons remain in Fighter Command.

1961 June–July: RAF FGA.9s at Bahrain help deter anticipated Iraqi invasion of Kuwait.

1963: Last two RAF Hunter F.6 squadrons begin re-equipping with the Lightning F.2.

1964–67: RAF Hunters operate against insurgents in the Yemen and Aden.

1964 20 February: four Hunter FGA.9s of 20 Squadron RAF fly surveillance and CAP in the ADIZ (Air Defence Identification Zone) encompassing North Borneo and Sarawak.

1964 August–September: RAF FGA.9s fly rocket and cannon firing strikes against Indonesian paratroops in Western Malaysia.

1964 May: RAF FGA.9s dislodge Indonesian insurgents with rocket- and cannon-strafing attacks.

1965 September: Indian Hunters take part in the Indo-Pakistani war.

1966 May: Six Hunters delivered to Saudi Arabia, thus paving the way for future massive arms deals.

1966 11 August: Indonesian confrontation ends. Hunters of the Iraqi and Jordan Air Forces used in the 'Six-Day War' against Israel.

1968 30 April: RAF Strike Command formed. Two NATO mobile FGA.9 squadrons form the tactical support and strike force.

1971: Last RAF FGA.9s withdrawn from first-line service.

1971 3–17 December: Second Indo-Pakistani conflict costs India twenty-two Hunters.

1971 June: Formation of two fully operational RAF Day Fighter/Ground Attack Hunter squadrons announced.

1971 October: Iraqi Hunters used in the Yom Kippur War with Israel.

1976 26 July: Nos 45 and 58 RAF Squadrons disbanded.

1994 March: Last operational RAF T.Mk 7s withdrawn.

1994 December: T.Mk 8s and GA.Mk 11s at FRADU at Yeovilton withdrawn. Switzerland retires the last of its Hunters.

1996: Indian Hunters retired from front-line service.